The Doll As Art

*Face, Form, and Fashion
in the Golden Age
of Dollmaking*

Stuart Holbrook

*Theriault's Gold Horse Publishing
Annapolis, Maryland*

Dedication

*To those who have overcome and found the courage to
create.*

Acknowledgments

*Many heartfelt thanks are extended to Susan Robinson for
her dedicated design work; George Theriault for creating
an atmosphere of success; and most of all to my mother,
Florence, for obvious reasons; to all whose lives have been
touched by hers.*

Printed in Hong Kong.

ISBN 0-912823-06-2

Preface

The doll has long been clustered into the mainstream of the collectibles market, associated with the likes of stamps, coins, and advertising memorabilia; yet, what of the doll as art - sensitive, mesmerizing - an idealized human portrait to haunt, tease, and fire the emotions of those who view it? Although the doll is a collectible in one sense, when argued that mass production and commercial profit was the goal of the early masters, who could also deny the individual artistry and romance which the doll portrays?

Could it be that dolls of the Golden Age, that is 1875-1920, elevate art to a new definitive plateau? There is little question when considering the depth of detail which each one possesses. The depth lies in a precise triad of artistry - face, form and fashion. Face - both painting and sculpting - molds the character of the subject. Form develops the shape and definition to create both movement and fluid visions. Fashion - the precise refinement of style - fosters the doll's individuality. The final culmination of this unique triad is the unquestionable glory of art.

As in all art forms, there was a geographical center of design, one which had a concentration of creative forces. For dolls, the epicenter extended from the always-influential art capital of Paris to the far reaches of the German forest of Thuringia. From 1870-1895 the choicest art forms were produced around Paris. However, the Paris design houses, overly concerned with precise details and artistry in their dolls became unprofitable ventures by 1895. By the time they saw a need for bi-level designs, that is, crafted works along with low-cost production dolls, it was too late. The dominance shifted at the turn of the century from Paris to Thuringia as a result of the downturn in quality, marketing, and production by the French. The Germans had stormed the world market with a perfect combination of attention to detail, individuality, and intelligent marketing.

With this very basic background of the shift of power during the Golden Age, the reader is able to understand a controversial issue which splits the doll market. Who created better dolls - the French or Germans? **The Doll as Art** *gives one the chance to visually assess the finest works from both countries and make an individual choice. It is important, though, to understand that whatever decision is reached, it is a personal one, and a matter of individual taste. Each period of dominance faced different social influences (a primary effect on doll design), and as such, had vastly different outcomes. For those who find pleasure in the whimsy of caricatures or fantasy themes no doubt the German dolls will be appealing; while at the same time, those who have a more romantic sense, will find the French bebes inevitably thrilling.*

The Doll as Art *is easily formatted for both aesthetics and ease of reference. Each of the two nations concerned have separate sections allowing a total vision of influence, style, and transition. The photographs are numbered to correspond with captions found at the end of the book, thereby, allowing for a more undisturbed view of these masterful objects. Finally, the captions themselves are more than just identification of maker and period, they focus on the previously-mentioned triad and assist in developing the reader's "eye" for quality.*

For those who are embarking on their first exposure to antique dolls, what follows will be an awakening to the beauty of the object as an art form. Perhaps, those who are actively involved, may soon embark on a renaissance of appreciation. Should this publication spark a new or rekindled meaning of "the doll as art," perhaps some will take time to consider acquiring their own gems, regardless of income, remembering that in the spectrum of prices experienced in the art world, dolls are still a bargain. To quote a lovely Victorian saying, "If I had but two loaves of bread, I would keep one to feed my hunger and sell one to buy white hyacinths to feed my soul."

The French Doll As Art

"If you should enter this hall and walk around in this corner of the gallery, take your time: go in the morning, because it is always full, full to bursting. Just imagine! This incomparable exhibit of toys of all sorts, each more ingenious than the next, is truly a childs' joy and a parents' tranquility. What astonishing nicknacks, music boxes, doll furniture; and what an astonishing collection of dolls. You don't have to have had children, nephews, nieces, or even god children to feel the money in your wallet get warm as you pass into that hall. The most popular cases with the crowd in this children's paradise are Bru Jne specialist in dolls and luxury bebes......"

From the Conty Guide to the 1878 Exposition in Paris relates the amazement of the public for the splendor of the new French dolls and toys.

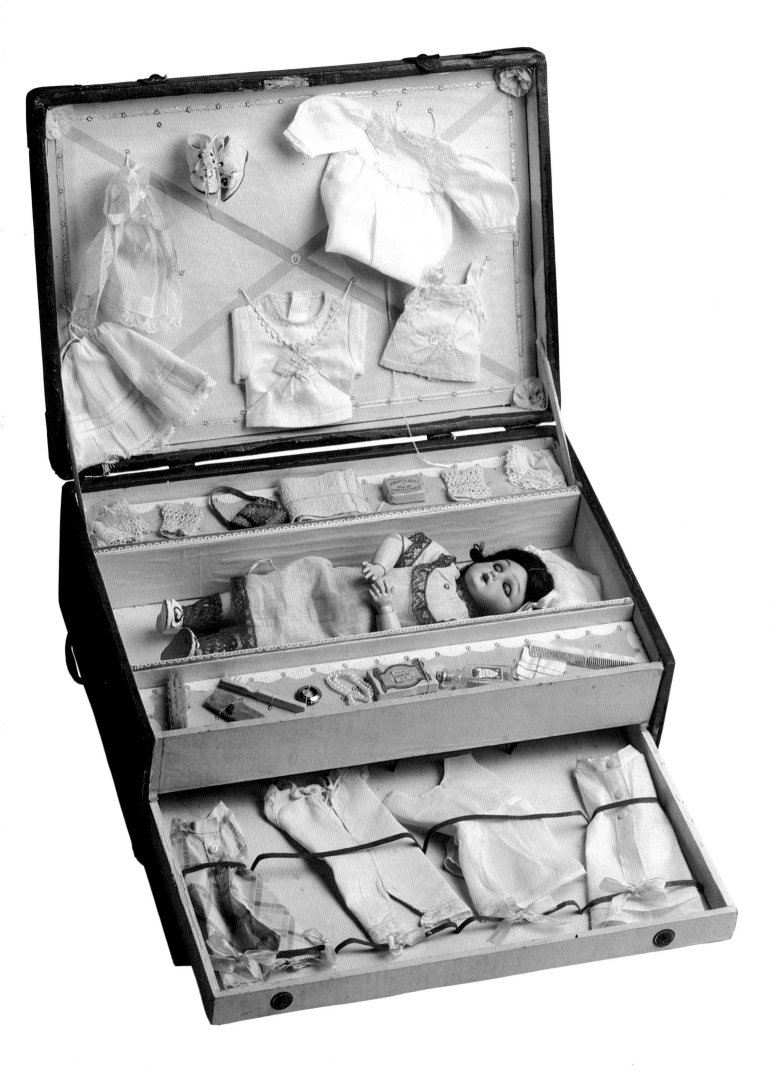

Jouet National

BÉBÉ JUMEAU

coiffé en cheveux naturels

Première Manufacture du Monde pour la Fabrication des Beaux Bébés

MAISON JUMEAU

Le Bébé Jumeau est le JOUET NATIONAL par excellence; il est partout, il a à toutes les grandes Expositions françaises et étrangères, pris a toujours obtenu un éclatant succès. Ses victoires ne se comptent plus, et dans ces luttes commerciales à l'argument contribué à propager en pays lointains la renommée de la fabrication française.

D'une fabrication extra supérieure, il est unique en son genre et absolument parfait, et il est non charmantes fillettes l'on adopté avec joie et bonheur, c'est qu'il réunit toutes les qualités indispensables à cette perfection: Beauté, Solidité, Légereté.

Le Bébé Jumeau est beau. — Il doit cette qualité à son heureux modèle exécuté par le gracieux maître statuaire Carrier-Belleuse, et sa tête, en fine porcelaine, possède un décor idéal qui la distingue de toutes les autres.

Le Bébé Jumeau est solide. — Il doit cette solidité à son genre de construction. Tous ses membres sont faits en bois de deux essences différentes, mortaisés et collés ensemble, ce qui les rend inséparables aux variations atmosphériques et empêchent de se fendiller.

Le Bébé Jumeau est léger. — Quoique solidement assemblés, tous ses membres, fait avec précision, cette légèreté est obtenue en enlevant aux membres une partie de leur poids par un creusement, fait avec précision, avant la réunion des deux bois nécessaires à leur construction.

Avec toutes ces qualités le Bébé Jumeau au premier rang de la fabrication française qui porte le nom de Jouet National.

GARANTIE
La tête du Bébé Jumeau a été reconnue propriété exclusive de la Maison Jumeau régulièrement et constamment par arrêt de la Cour d'Appel de Paris.

DÉPOT
La forme de son nouveau corps a été déposée au Conseil des Prud'hommes.

Dans leur carton, les Bébés sont toujours placés les pieds du côté de l'étiquette extérieure.

LE BÉBÉ JUMEAU EST VENDU PAR LES MAISONS DE PREMIER ORDRE

Toujours les 1res Récompenses

The German Doll As Art

*"For the first time, Mr. Jumeau, the Roi de poupees,
as he called himself, visited the fair and he achieved
unexpected good results. Mr. Jumeau might have smiled
about the prices of his German competitors, his lot was
still a better one. He obtains prices about which we can be
nothing else than astonished. However, as far as his taste
is concerned, it is in our opinion, too baroque and exceeds
the understanding of even the most fastidious child."*

A quote from Phillip
Samhammer of Sonneberg,
German doll factory owner and
writer for the *Berliner Zeitung,*
on the 1887 Leipzig Toy Fair
and the controversial visit of
Emile Jumeau.

*"We are proud to have caused the doll industry to flourish
again with our character doll."*

Franz Reinhardt of the Kammer
and Reinhardt firm 1910.

Description and Commentary

30. French fashion "Rose Stebbins," mystery maker, circa 1870. An inventory included with the doll names her as "Rose Stebbins" from a Boston family and highlights the importance of provenance in improving the desirability of a doll even in cases of unknown makers such as this. Included is original trunk and wardrobe.

31. French twin bebes, mystery maker, circa 1880. Wonderful pair of early closed-mouth bebes are beautifully costumed in appropriate fashions and are contained in original trunk labelled "Debauve & Gallois/Paris."

32-33. Ten French bisque "Tete" models by Emile Jumeau, circa 1885. By grouping these various-sized "Tete" Jumeau, one is able to note the vast difference in facial painting and modelling used for the Jumeau company's most successfully marketed doll - proof of dolls as an individual art form rather than a production item.

34. French bisque "Triste" by Emile Jumeau, circa 1885. The doll produced for the longest period by Emile Jumeau, the rare "Triste" is a tribute to this firm's creature force. The dolls are characterized by long modelling of face, delicate brush strokes in the decoration, and a look of shy sensitivity.

35. French mystery portrait man, circa 1910, with French fashion lady by Gaultier, circa 1875. The rare male portrait doll is probably by S.F.B.J. and aptly depicts pensive-faced adult wearing original black formal suit. The Parisienne has beautiful modelling and bisque and is also well-costumed.

36. French bebe by Albert Marque for S.F.B.J., circa 1915. Without any question, the delicate urchin child created by legendary sculptor, Albert Marque, for the S.F.B.J. company was the pinnacle of artistry in dolls. Unique molding, deep facial sculpting and perhaps the finest painting ever, combined to make this spectacular bebe a legend with collectors today. The use of a noted French sculptor by a doll company also shows the parallel between art and dolls.

37. French bebe "SX," mystery maker, circa 1890. A most unusual bebe in that little is known regarding its origins. The design verges on a character expression highlighting the emergence of personality in French Bebes regardless of their lack of success.

38. French bebe by Jumeau, circa 1880. Wonderful personality is portrayed in the tiny bebe with original frock showing traces of Jumeau label.

39. French bisque child doll, Jumeau, circa 1875. An "E.J." model as originally costumed and displayed by Mlle. Nadaud who displayed dolls at Paris Exposition in 1878. Petite cabinet doll in superb unplayed-with condition, wears antique brown leather shoes marked "Bru Jne Paris," original muslin and silk pleated chemise, matching red maroon silk ribbons and has second muslin and embroidered frock.

40. Pair of French "E.J." bebes by Jumeau, circa 1880. Elegance in costume design, rare large size and perfection in painting make these two models of the "E.J." by Jumeau quite extraordinary.

41. French fashion by Blampoix, circa 1870, and French "Bebe Teteur" by Casimir Bru, circa 1880. This majestic Parisienne lady by the obscure firm of Aine Blampoix is dramatized by brilliant eyes, large size and lavish antique lace frock. The Bru Teteur or Nursing Bru retains especially lovely quality and is a fine example of the many unique Bru patents as it actually utilizes a hand mechanism to allow a bottle to be sucked.

42. French fashion, maker unknown, circa 1870. Serene portrait model has loveliest pale bisque enhanced by dramatic cornflower blue eyes.

43. Pair of French characters by Emile Jumeau, circa 1890. How ironic to this transition period of dollmaking that Jumeau's most imaginative and beautifully-sculpted creations would become commercial disasters and turn the tide on the downfall of the Jumeau House.

44. French bebe by Mothereau, circa 1880. While a considerably smaller doll firm compared to the likes of Gaultier, the Mothereau House produced a series of wonderful bebes usually with overly-expressive eyes as seen here.

45. French bebe by Louis Schneider, circa 1880. So few dolls are encountered by this little-known artist that collectors are often confused by the "S.L." mark which they possess (simply the artist's initials in reverse). While somewhat obscure, it stands tribute to the superb craftsmanship of the many smaller "cottage companies" blossoming in France during this period.

46. French bebe by Rabery and Delphieu, circa 1885. A very choice model by this mid-size firm in unusually large size has exemplary quality of modelling including pertly-shaped lips and chin, delicate blushing on palest bisque.

47. Pair of French bebes by Casimir Bru, circa 1880. One sees here an interesting contrast in size between the petite model by Bru and the rare, possibly one-of-a-kind mannequin model. On the larger Bru, it is possible to truly appreciate the depth of artistry, an almost human look, which Casimir Bru created so often.

48. French bisque automaton with Jumeau head attributed to Roullet et Decamps, circa 1885. Automatons must be judged not only for the quality of appearance, but for the intricacy and fluidity of movement which they possess as in this wonderful all-original example.

49. French bebe by Schmitt, circa 1885. Compare painting and sculpting to Photograph No. 11.

50. French bebe by Jumeau, circa 1885. Exemplary oily bisque enhances the deep decoration of lashes and eyeshadow. Perhaps the most special characteristic, though, is the tremendous exhibition costume of maroon velvet with gilt braid and buttons, original matching gilt label "Bebe Jumeau" on sleeve.

51. French bebe by mystery maker, circa 1885. Simply known as the "Mariner Girl," obviously referring to the original costume. There is little provenance to associate the lovely and expressive doll to any one maker. The inscription on the cap "L'Espiegle" translates into "Mischievous."

52. French bebe "A" series by Jules Steiner, circa 1885. Spectacular large size of the rare bebe has wonderfully-appealing expression, soft rose complexion, and choice decoration of bisque.

53. French lady doll by Emile Jumeau, circa 1880. This seldom-seen adult portrait by Jumeau is perhaps one of the finest sculpted lady dolls ever created in this period. The oddly-shaped eyes, deeply-sculpted chin and wonderfully-contrasted painting make her a true masterpiece.

54. French fashion, mystery maker, circa 1870. A gentle-featured Parisienne lady wears frail original silk frock and has choicest delicate bisque.

55. Pair of French portrait bebes, one by mystery maker, one by Schmitt et Fils, circa 1880. The antique maroon gabardine wool dress beautifully sets off the shy-faced features on this petite bebe. The Schmitt retains exquisite pale bisque and decoration with entrancing threaded eyes and all-original costume.

56. French bisque by Petit et Dumoutier, circa 1885. Known simply as the "P.D.," this rare bebe transcends the sensuality of the typical French bebe and creates a beautiful crossbreed of innocence and personality.

57. French character by S.F.B.J., circa 1912. Outstanding example of the rare character urchin, a series created by one of the last of the French firms to compete with German characters dominating this period of production. The pouty toddler has a most fetching expression enhanced by choicest oily patina and delicate coloring.

58. Pair of French bebes by Schmitt, circa 1885. Compare to Photograph Nos. 11 and 49, noting the different look of the petite model. This couple is particularly lovely in the matching silk costumes.

59. French bebe by Casimir Bru, circa 1885. Few bebes of this period were produced with black coloring and, as such, are quite sought after by collectors. While having all the characteristics of modelling as other Bru's, the black version seen here has superb quality of painting of dark tones and an all-original wardrobe.

60. French bebe by Gaultier, circa 1885. Once again, the unique modelling of the jowls are prevalent in this spectacular model of the Gaultier bebe.

61. French "C" series bebe by Jules Steiner, circa 1880. This entrancing character-look of the rare French "C" series Steiner is evident as is the nicely-contrasted painting of cheeks and the uniquely-expressive mouth.

62-63. French bebe by Thuillier, circa 1880. Elegantly garbed in its original French couturier costume, this "A.T." can be considered one of the finest examples known. Examine the detail in sketching and the original labels as shown in the inset photograph. Compare the detail in painting with the previous models shown in Photograph Nos. 15 and 21.

64. French bebe "Triste" by Jumeau, circa 1885. Typical modelling and quality for the Jumeau Triste, yet, this example benefits by its original box and tremendous couturier costume.

65. A choice all-original Lioret "Bebe Phonographe" by Jumeau, circa 1890. Impeccable condition of this choice and rare doll, contained unplayed-with in its original box with detailed instructions in French, Spanish, and English, the doll wears original floral-sprigged dress with front flap for access in changing discs, original earrings and No. 11 Jumeau shoes.

66. French characters by Poulbot for S.F.B.J., circa 1913. Once again, here is proof of the crossover between Parisien artists and doll production. The artist, Poulbot, is legendary in designing propaganda posters depicting starving street children in Paris during the first World War. Here he was contracted, as was Albert Marque, to design dolls for S.F.B.J.

67. French adult portrait by Casimir Bru, circa 1885. Casimir Bru produced a limited number of portraits of an African tribal leader in his traditional clothing. Unique in artistic sensitivity, the doll has a tremendous provenance and comes with sixteen layers of original clothing and even a traditional mudpack hairpiece.

68. French bebe "Tete" model by Jumeau, circa 1880. This rare-sized petite bebe wears her very elaborate exhibition costume of ivory brocade trimmed with gilt braid and original armband with gilt letters "Bebe Jumeau" setting its steps higher than a typical, rather common, Tete model.

69. French bebe "B.F.," circa 1896. Abbreviated for "Bebe Francais," the B.F. doll was trademarked by both Danel et Cie and Jumeau, yet, the "Medaille d'or" designation indicates Jumeau production. Incidentally, Danel was a former artist of the Jumeau House evidence of the fascinating, sometimes controversial, history which gravitated around doll artists.

70-71. French "Tete" bebe by Jumeau, circa 1889. While a relatively common doll, this Tete model portrays both a fascinating provenance and tremendous couturier designs. The doll was originally raffled off by a society womens group in Pittsburgh in the late 1800's and was fitted with 11 additional costumes all designed by leading French couturier houses. Truly a remarkable design in the sense of history and fashion.

72. French bebe by Gaultier, circa 1885. Compare the facial expressions and painting to previous "F.G." models and note the difference in quality between this petite model and the larger, more expressive creations. Whatever is lacking in comparitive quality is made up in the charm of its cabinet size and originality.

73. French fashion, maker unknown, circa 1870. An additional fashion of porcelain which is attributed, yet not confirmed, to the doll artistry of Madame Rohmer. Typical of the Rohmer dolls is the superb quality of the porcelain and deeply-painted cheeks.

74. Pair of French bebe "portraits" by Emile Jumeau, circa 1880. Tremendous artistry in these early matching portrait bebes by Jumeau beautifully complemented by early elaborate costumes.

75. French fashion by Gaultier, circa 1885. While the facial artistry is typical of the early Gaultier fashions, its larger size and wonderful original costume combine for a near-perfect example.

76. A trio of French dolls and automata, circa 1875-1885. Pictured are a lovely pair of fashion dolls by the master, Casimir Bru, both possessing gentle smiling and serene expressions. The automaton is a rare Vichy "Girl on Scooter" giving example of the tremendous mechanical artistry which was blended with dolls to create movement and further human expression.

77. *French automaton by Vichy, circa 1885. Another excellent example of the mechanical works of Gustave Vichy, utilizing a bisque head by Gaultier. Extraordinary original condition is retained on this keywound masterpiece.*

78. *French bebe by Casimir Bru, circa 1875. Outstanding quality and condition of the rare large model Bru bebe, further enhanced by an original photographic provenance.*

79. *French bebe "D" series by Steiner, circa 1885. While detail to painting is rather mediocre, the "D" Steiner is best noted for its unusual expression and rarity.*

80-81. *Five French Fashion lady dolls by Casimir Bru, circa 1870. By arranging a grouping of fashions by the Bru firm one is able to garnish a respect for the diversity and creativity each model possesses. Especially note the variations in neck construction, body styles, and modelling of the eyes and mouth.*

82. *Introduction to German Dolls*

83. *German characters 107 and 109 by Kammer and Reinhardt, circa 1912. Two rare character dolls by the firm most noted and regarded for fine, unusual portraits of children. The K*R firm, as it is often referred to, has utilized unusual slender modelling for the 107 model giving the appearance of a perfect German boy and softened the girl by expressing deep, pouty modelling. Notice the intriguing use of intaglio eyes which K*R crafted on their character series.*

84. *Pair of German bisque dolls by Kestner, circa 1890-1915. A contrast of production time is evident when examining the early closed-mouth doll by the prolific firm of Kestner, circa 1890, and the large character baby "Hilda," circa 1915. This 35 year period brought great transitions of style in dollmaking in Germany, proving not only their creative spirit but also their sensitivity to the needs of the market.*

85. *Pair of German characters by Gebruder Heubach, circa 1912. While not the rarest of dolls by this diverse porcelain firm, the pair of character babies have the benefit of a complete provenance including photos of the owners as children and correspondence regarding their ownership.*

86. *German portrait of Oriental 1329 by Simon and Halbig, circa 1910. Very choice quality of bisque and decoration on the rare portrait.*

87. *German portrait of Oriental 1329 by Simon and Halbig, circa 1910. Compare with Photograph No. 86. This exhibition model of the exquisitely-costumed Oriental lady is all-original, the uniquely-constructed body with shortened arms effectively displays the distinctive sleeve costume of the unmarried Chinese girl.*

88. *Pair of German characters 112 and 101 by K*R, circa 1912. The character boy 112 is not only a seldom-seen model, but as in this example can be found with glass eyes instead of intaglio, adding to its rarity. Note the deep sculpting and expressive detail especially around the chin area and nose of both portraits.*

89. *Early German child, maker unknown, circa 1885. Beautiful character model with somber expression enhanced by ivory-like bisque, dramatic dark eyes and all-original provincial costume.*

90. *German portrait by Kestner, circa 1890. This wonderful portrait stands tribute to the tremendous early work of the German artists even during French dominance in the doll market. The gentle brush-strokes, thick eyebrows, and shy expression are similar to French dolls of the period yet retain a sense of German artistry.*

91. *German child by Kestner, circa 1880. A very beautiful early closed-mouth doll has original body and wig, flawless bisque. Included is paper-covered trunk containing accessories and wardrobe made for the doll by the original owner.*

92. *German baby 126 by Kammer and Reinhardt, circa 1915. The pristine baby, in unplayed-with condition, is presented in an extraordinary and all-original wicker layette with elaborate arrangement of clothes, blanket and toys. The layette indubitably produced for a luxury boutique and incredibly preserved.*

93. *German character 153 by Simon and Halbig, circa 1912. The artistic influence of Kammer and Reinhardt on other German firms, even one as established and creative as Simon and Halbig, can be seen on numerous dolls, such as this S&H 153 boy. The character portrait is stunning, with its sculpted hair and somewhat pensive expression.*

94. *Pair of German character "Hilda" babies by Kestner, circa 1912. The use of varying form creates vastly-different images of the same doll. A portrait of a young child is formed by implementing a toddler body and then that of a baby is created by using a baby body.*

95. *German character 149 by Hertel & Schwab, circa 1912. Recently, research has shown that many dolls previously considered unknown or falsely attributed were produced by the somewhat obscure firm of Hertel and Schwab. Only now, are connoisseurs of German works appreciative of the fine craftsmanship that this influential factory was capable of, as seen in this 149 model which possesses wonderful sculpting of the lips and superb painting of features.*

96. *German character child 1279 by Simon and Halbig, circa 1910. A rare model has exquisite delicate bisque and well-sculpted details. Note the distinctive accent dot on the lower lip.*

97. *German child by Franz Schmidt, circa 1915. A very rare and wonderful laughing coquette has choicest bisque and decoration, wonderful personality, exceptional modelling of body.*

98. *German character "Fany" by Armand Marseille, circa 1912. While generally associated with non-art production dolls of common abundance the Armand Marseille company did retain artists to produce a limited number of find character dolls as in the trademark model "Fany."*

99. *German fashion lady by Simon and Halbig with all bisque mystery maker, circa 1880. The Germans also utilized the artistry of lady dolls during the peak period of French doll market dominance. This early model by S&H has lovely pale bisque contrasted with deep coloring of the cheeks. Expression on the German fashions was generally more pronounced. Seated in the lovely Victorian wheelchair in miniature is an early all bisque, maker unknown, yet outstanding in its features and petite artistry.*

100. Assortment of German character babies by Grace Storey Putnam, circa 1923. While quite common in the antiquities market, the "Bye-lo" baby by Grace Storey Putnam was, without question, a formidable work of art. Excellent painting, cherub-like complexions, and adoring facial artistry make them an attractive item regardless of their lack of scarcity.

101. Pair of German "OIC" character babies by Kestner, circa 1914. Though considered by some to be unattractive and exaggerated, there is no doubting the uniqueness of the OIC baby. The finest of modelling is achieved in the expressive mouth and tongue.

102. German character 109 "Elise" by Kammer and Reinhardt, circa 1911. A portrait of unsurpassed perfection is the "Elise" model. Due to its complete artistic fullness, original clothing, ethnic flavor, and beautiful modelling and painting, the genius of Kammer and Reinhardt is firmly planted in the forefront of German doll companies.

103. German portrait 1308 by Simon and Halbig, circa 1910. A very rare character model aptly depicts smiling older man, wears original costume.

104. German character 101 "Marie" by Kammer and Reinhardt. While relatively common in todays character market the Marie model proves that Kammer and Reinhardt could utilize high production to meet demand yet retain a distinct and impeccable level of quality.

105. German character baby by Kestner, circa 1912. A previously undocumented model, this possible one-of-a-kind infant portrait possesses unique sculpting of hair, deeply modelled features and sculpted mouth.

106. German character "150" by Simon & Halbig, circa 1912. This seldom seen character doll is beautifully preserved in original Scottish costume. Typical modelling includes deeply sculpted features, expressive intaglio eyes and delicate subtle painting.

107. German character toddler by Bahr and Proschild, circa 1915. Extremely charming doll with a less then serious expression, somewhat full-faced modelling and deeply painted cheeks. A typical light hearted doll by this and many German firms of the time.

108. German character baby "Hilda" by Kestner, circa 1914. A tremendously popular doll with collectors, perhaps for its expressive and jovial look. The Hilda comes in numerous variations including this rare black example.

109. German character "1301" by Simon & Halbig, circa 1912. This haunting and exotic character by S&H is testament to their unsurpassed work in creating unique ethnic models. The features, though somewhat exaggerated, remain dramatic and alluring. Perfect deep black complexion is the finishing touch to this extraordinary doll.

110. German character series by Kestner, circa 1914. While Kestner was not particularly known for producing painted eyes of the K*R type dolls, certain models do exist. Of these probably most often seen are the 180 series which have choice complexion and full modelling of the cheeks along with variations in expression.

111. German bisque Fashion lady by Simon & Halbig, circa 1875. Compare to S&H fashion photographed on pg 99. This model retains far more delicate features and the benefit of a swivel neck. The contrast between facial and cheek painting is also not so drastically featured giving it a softer appeal. The elaborate coiffure is further enhancement to this already exceptional doll.

112. German character 106 by Kammer and Reinhardt, circa 1910. Perhaps the perfect blend of rarity and artistry is achieved on the 106 model giving way to its tremendous desirability in today's market. Few models were produced for exhibitions and toy fairs, never to be totally marketed. How unfortunate for this lack of early popularity when admiring the deep modelling lines, especially in the prominent chin, the beautifully sculpted lips and the overall choice quality of the bisque.

113. German bisque "141" by Hertel and Schwab, circa 1912. The rare model has exceptional detail of modelling, choice decoration and bisque and most appealing characterization. Also exceptional are the lovely intaglio eyes.

114. German character "243" by Kestner circa 1914. Oriental dolls were quite popular during the golden age and normally were finished off with elaborate and closely authentic costumes. The J.D.K. oriental baby pictured here comes in its original costume labeled "Gump's Department Store", San Francisco. One variation of the "243" is a painted hair model, which is far scarcer.

115. German child by mystery maker, circa 1900. Earlier ethnic depictions such as this Sonnenbourg doll appeared after 1880, due to the European fascination with Orientals and dark complexions. The Germans later perfected the art as seen in this tremendous representation of an Oriental child with perfect complexion and subtle Eastern modelling.

116. Pair German characters "123" and "124" by Kammer & Reinhardt, circa 1914. Perhaps the most beloved of the K*R 100 series. "Max and Moritz" were the direct influence of the German cartoon strip whose U.S. counterpart was "The Katzenjammer Kids." Extraordinary whimsy is seen in the modelling of the dimples, painting of the eyebrows and the watermelon smile.

117. German character "1329" by Simon and Halbig, circa 1910. Another choice example of Simon Halbig's exceptional ethnic production, the Eskimo child has lovely amber tinted complexion enhanced by dark eye decoration and oily patina. She wears original Eskimo costume of white fur.

118. German child "939" by Simon and Halbig, circa 1890. A highly successful and beautifully designed model by S&H has most appealing pouty expression with rarer closed mouth and beautifully defined features. Especially thick eye brows are found on this model with flattened dome, erroneously called Belton by collectors.

119. *Pair of German child dolls by Kestner, circa 1885. Further proof is shown of Kestner's dominance over other German firms in the design and production of early closed mouth models. As usual, gorgeous coloring and detailed painting prevails on these charming dolls.*

120. *German character child by Gebruder Heubach, circa 1914. This exceptionally rare laughing child by Heubach projects a jovial look with its humorous design, especially the modelling of the mouth. Along side is a German celluloid squeeze toy, circa 1915.*

121. *Pair of German characters "520" by Kley and Hahn, circa 1910. More known for "dolly face" dolls and babies the K&H firm rarely produced characters, especially those which possess such quality and originality. These companion dolls retain realistically modelled expressions, especially in the subtle smile. In addition, the wonderful bisque and choice original costumes help to make these examples rare and appealing.*

122. *German character "100" by Kammer and Reinhardt, circa 1910. Often referred to as the "Kaiser baby", the 100 model by K&R was the first of their illustrious character line. Normally designed with painted eyes, the glass eyed model seen here is quite rare and normally commands five times the value.*

123. *German character "Baby Jean" by Kestner, circa 1912. Once again Kestner designs a most unique and expressive baby. Wonderful modelling of the mouth and superb painting of the hair give this an especially nice appeal. Choice decoration and lovely costume are additional benefits to this popular model.*

124. *German character child by Bahr and and Proschild, circa 1912. This rarely found character doll retains a wonderful expression with deeply-modelled features, choice bisque and detailed decoration. The child is further enhanced by a dramatic original costume.*

125. *German character "323" by Armand Marseille, circa 1915. Although primarily recognized for producing large quantities of mediocre, inexpensive bisque dolls, the A.M. company successfully created a limited selection of high quality, unique character dolls such as this trademarked example. While the bodies are of the typical poor Marseille quality the head is a wonderfully designed "googly" with especially fine detail to the modelling of the mouth.*

126. *German character "6969" by Gebruder Heubach, circa 1912. Coveted today by collectors as one of the finest examples of "pouty" doll production, the 6969 is no doubt one of Heubach's most successful and influential dolls. Normally this character retains a wonderful deep coloring and dramatic modelling of the tender and sad face. Note the fine, perfect brushstrokes for the eye lashes.*

127. *Pair of German characters "Max and Moritz" by Recknagel, circa 1914. Once again the tremendous popularity of these fun-loving cartoon characters resulted in a pair of dolls, this time by the somewhat small firm of Recknagel. Vastly different from the K&R interpretation shown earlier, these examples have humorous molded hair and wonderfully comic expressions.*

128. *German character toddler "220" by Kestner, circa 1915. The rare doll has choicest bisque enhancing the very deep sculptured features, splendid oily patina of complexion, and a rarer toddler body.*

129. *German child doll by Kestner, circa 1880. The delicate complexion is beautifully blended with the lush painting of the cheeks and the thick eyebrows. The child has typical superb quality of the closed mouth Kestners.*

130. *German character "117" by Kammer and Reinhardt, circa 1912. So called "Mein Liebling", the 117 model by K*R is a superb example of transition dollmaking from character to "dolly face." Normal artistry includes soft painting and modelling, glass eyes and either open or closed mouth. Flirty eyes are sometimes also found.*

131. *German character "1388" by Simon and Halbig, circa 1912. Obviously inspired by Charles Dana Gibsons illustrations of the Victoria Gibson girl, this lady creatively surges forth with a unique, almost comic expression. Note the flirty eyes which are prevalent to all "1300" series dolls by S&H. Further detail includes lady body and elaborate victorian costume.*

132. *German character "8678" by Gebruder Heubach, circa 1920. A splendid composition by this noted character doll firm. Excellent character representation is beautifully complemented by a stunning, original cossack costume.*

133. *German character "131" by Kammer and Reinhardt, circa 1912. It seems every doll company of the period had at least one "googly", referring to the whimsical eyes, in their line of character dolls. No doubt that K*R, the innovator of all German character dolls, would design the most expressive! Charming watermelon smile and well painted features make this a comical work of art.*

134. *German character "Klein Mammi", by Kammer and Reinhardt. One of K*Rs' later models from the 100 series. This, the number 171, was an attempt for the now declining firm to catch up with the baby doll craze of the 20's. Few were ever made. The rare doll has rich detail of modelling around the eyes and mouth and beautifully featured hair.*

135. *German character "Baby Stuart" by Gebruder Heubach, circa 1912. One of Heubach's more imaginative creations, the so-called "Baby Stuart" was created in numerous variations. This, a particularly unusual model has removable bisque bonnet, glass eyes and superb painting of the cap.*